BIOGRAPHIES FOR KIDS

All about Rosa Parks:
The Civil Rights Movement of America

Children's Biographies of Famous People Books

BABY PROFESSOR
EDUCATION KIDS

Speedy Publishing LLC
40 E. Main St. #1156
Newark, DE 19711
www.speedypublishing.com
Copyright 2015

WHO IS ROSA PARKS?

WHAT DID SHE DO TO INFLUENCE THE AMERICAN CIVIL RIGHTS MOVEMENT?

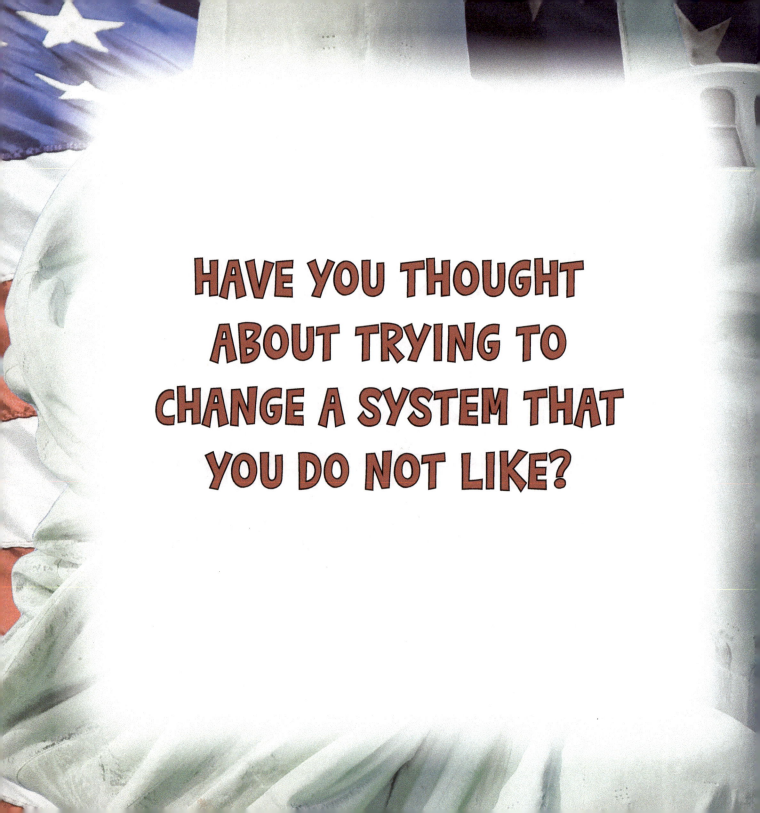

HAVE YOU THOUGHT ABOUT TRYING TO CHANGE A SYSTEM THAT YOU DO NOT LIKE?

WHAT QUALITIES SHOULD YOU HAVE TO IMPLEMENT GREAT CHANGE IN THE COMMUNITY?

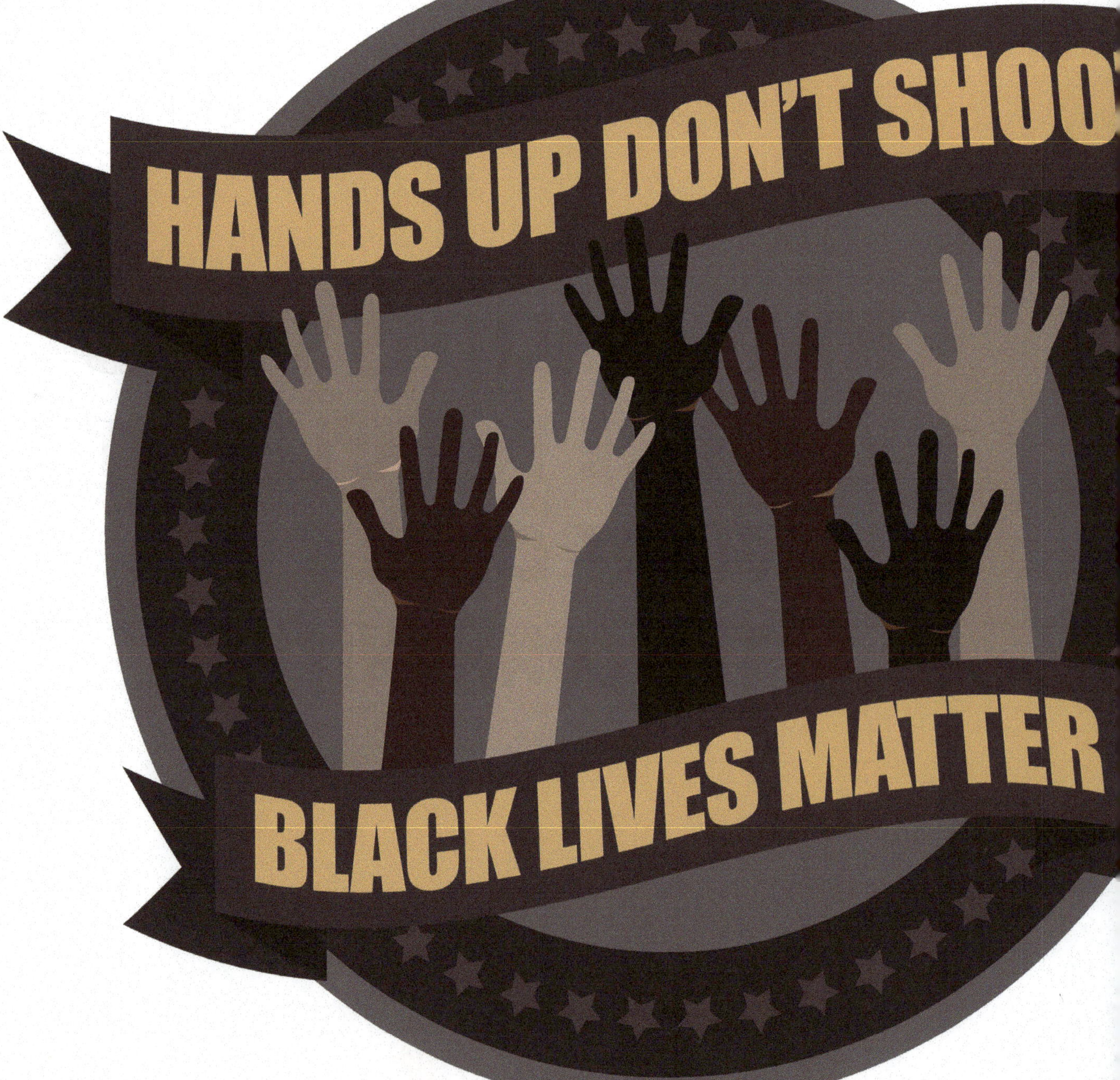

HANDS UP DON'T SHOO
BLACK LIVES MATTER

BE BRAVE LIKE ROSA PARKS

It was on December 1, 1955 that an unforgettable moment in America happened.

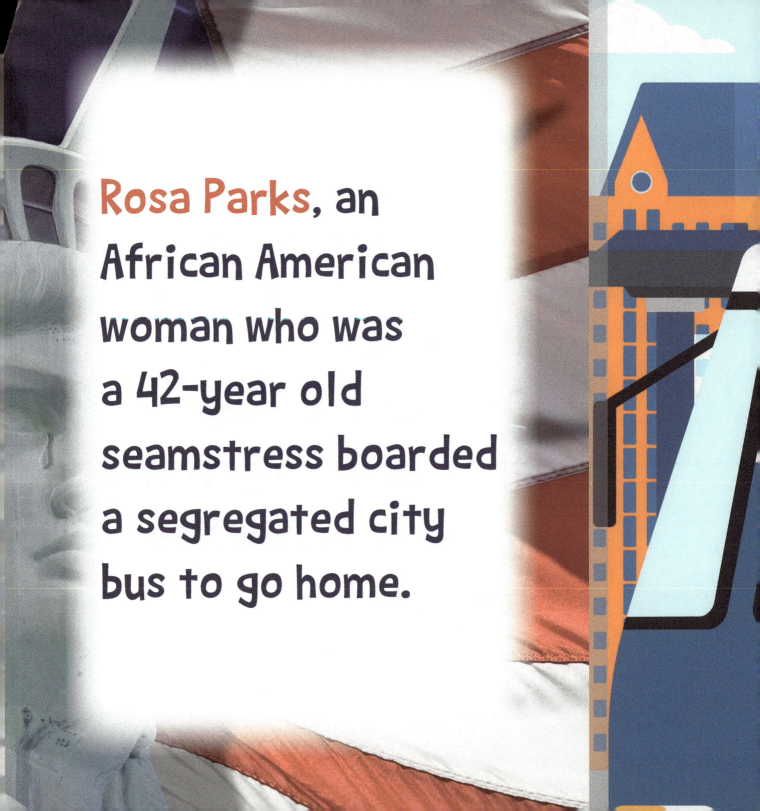

Rosa Parks, an African American woman who was a 42-year old seamstress boarded a segregated city bus to go home.

She refused to give up her seat to a White man when the bus became full.

She was ordered by the bus driver to give her seat. But Rosa firmly refused to do so and stayed in her seat.

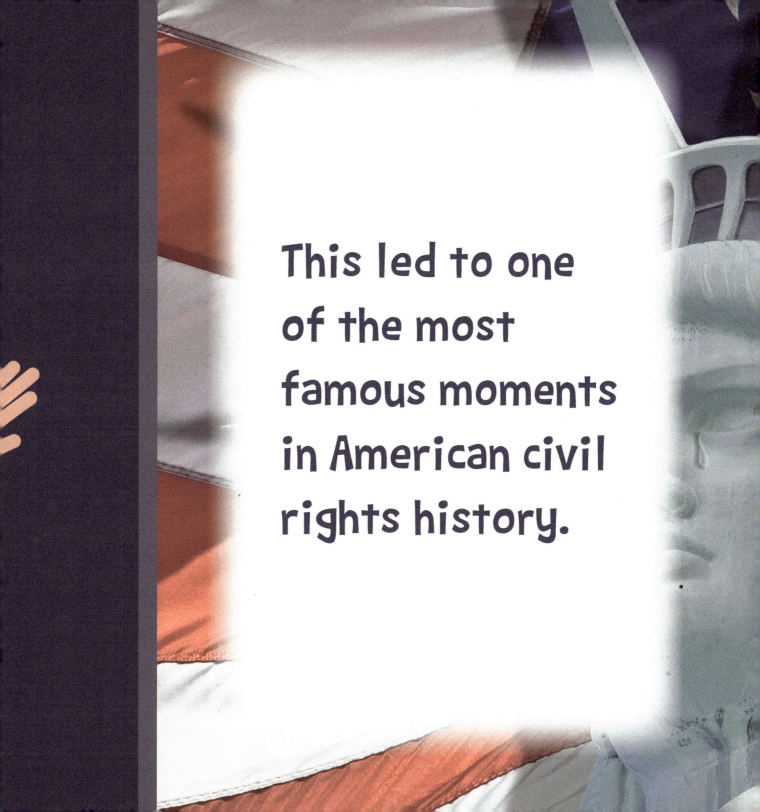

This led to one of the most famous moments in American civil rights history.

According to Segregation laws, blacks were mandated to give up their seats when there were no seats available on the bus and a white person got on the bus,

So by not giving up her seat, Rosa Parks defied the norms of the society where she lived.

Breaking the existing laws of segregation required great strength and courage which lead to her arrest.

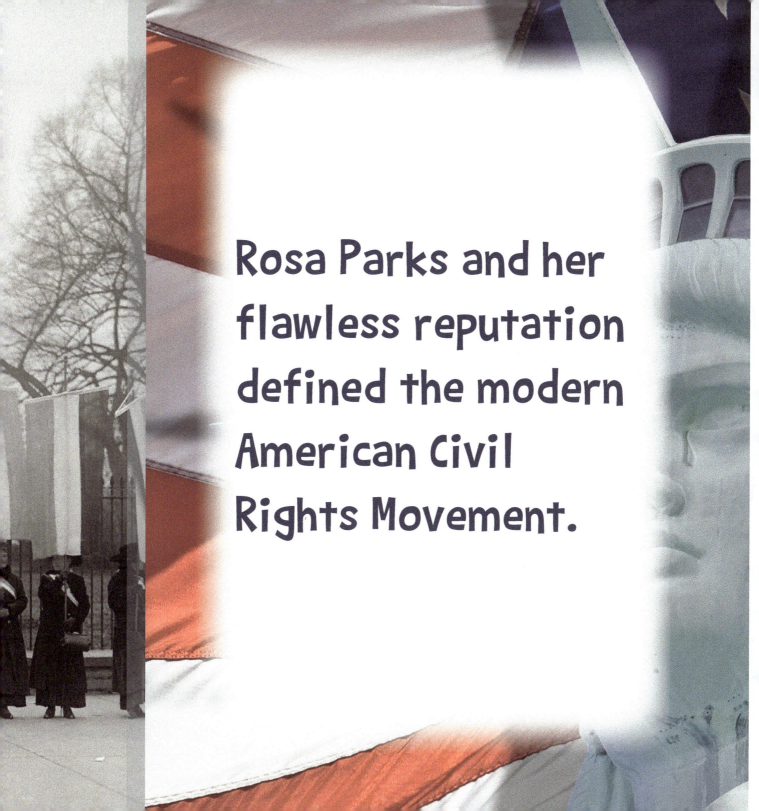

Rosa Parks and her flawless reputation defined the modern American Civil Rights Movement.

Rosa Park's meaningful act sparked a social transformation.

This somewhat changed the racial relations in America. But it was noted that there were other black women who fought back before Rosa Parks.

These were Susie McDonald, Aurelia Browder, Mary Louise Smith and Claudette Colvin. All of them were allegedly arrested on buses in Montgomery for challenging the law.

But Rosa Park's defiance of the segregation law was seen as different and unique. Her arrest brought the community to act and respond.

Her innate personality brought this climactic change in American civil rights history.

Her flawless character, inner strength and fortitude inspired the boycott of black people using the public buses in Montgomery which lasted 381 days.

This was considered the largest demonstration against the Segregation Law.

As a result, the boycott made the US Supreme Court to recall the segregation law on public buses in Alabama.

Moreover, nonviolent protests became evident in many other cities. Then Martin Luther King Jr., a young Baptist minister became the leader of the civil rights movement.

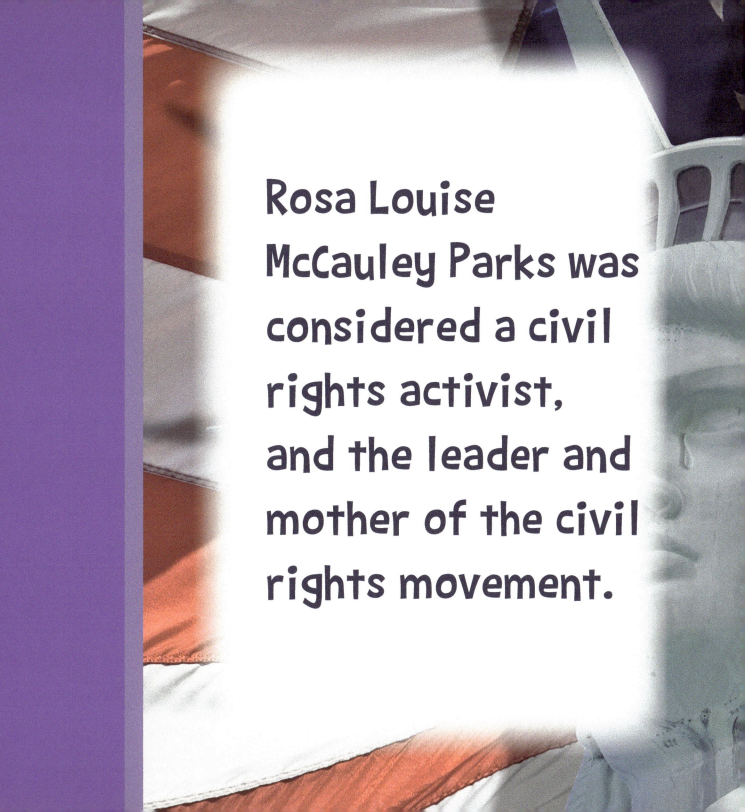

Rosa Louise McCauley Parks was considered a civil rights activist, and the leader and mother of the civil rights movement.

Her meaningful act to achieve fair justice and racial relations prompted the Civil Rights of 1964 and the Voting Rights Act of 1965.

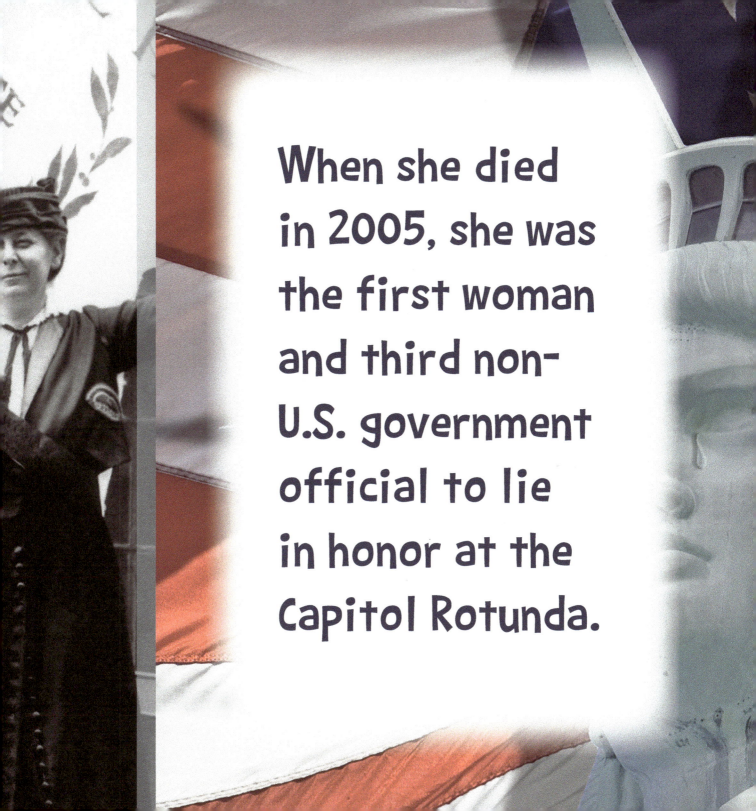

When she died in 2005, she was the first woman and third non-U.S. government official to lie in honor at the Capitol Rotunda.

WHAT ROSA PARK DID WAS A HUGE SOCIAL REVOLUTION IN MODERN AMERICAN HISTORY.

DO YOU KNOW SOMEONE AS BRAVE AS ROSA PARK?

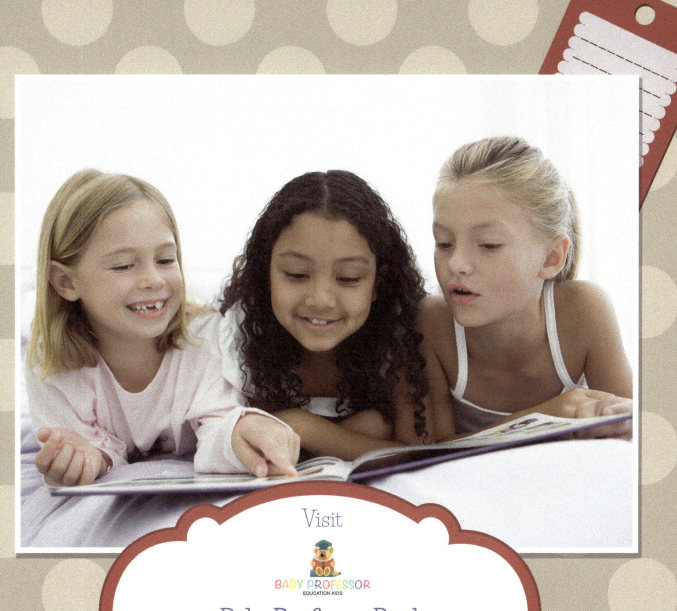

Visit

BABY PROFESSOR
EDUCATION KIDS

www.BabyProfessorBooks.com

to download Free Baby Professor eBooks
and view our catalog of new and exciting
Children's Books

Lightning Source UK Ltd.
Milton Keynes UK
UKHW050059300519

343562UK00006B/26/P